First Printing, 2018
V2 Mini

Published by:
Lara Willing
www.larawilling.com
www.3ThingsJournal.com

Cover by Tera Antaree

ISBN-13:
978-1717544988

ISBN-10:
1717544983

Mini

3 Things Journal

by Lara Willing

and YOU!

© Lara Willing 2018

I will be donating a portion of all proceeds
to the Human Awareness Institute (HAI Global)
to support the wonderful work
they do around the world and
to express my gratitude for
all the ways they have enriched my life.
www.HAI.org

Acknowledgements

To my clients, who inspire and teach me every day.

To my friends, family, and HAI community for all the ways you hold me.

To my closest circle - Michael, Mary, Christine, Margaret, Aaron, Todd, Lisa, Mike, and Barbara:
Thank you for being on this journey with me.

And, of course, to Gordo, who is and will always be with me.

Welcome to your
Mini 3 Things Journal !

I invite you to use this journal to create a few minutes of self-care whenever you open it.

There are no rules or shoulds. You can use this journal however you want to!

Some people will diligently write in this journal every day. Others will read and write in it when they feel the urge.

Some will answer prompts with a word or two, others will use every bit of white space to write.

Some will skip around and find prompts they like. Others will look at only one page at a time and leave each new page to be a surprise.

This journal is your space, to do with as you please. However you do it is perfect! Whatever you do, please don't use this as an(other?) opportunity to beat yourself up!

My hope is that your time with this journal will open your heart and your mind and give you an opportunity to reflect on your life. Most of all, I hope it feels good doing this for yourself. Happy journaling!

— Lara

Visit www.3ThingsJournal.com !

Important tip:

You can get this journal spiral bound for just a few dollars at your local print shop. Then it will lie flat.

(Publishing it spiral bound is really expensive)

©Lara Willing 2017

3 things for which I am grateful

-
-
-

3 things I am excited about

-
-
-

Run from what is
comfortable. Forget safety.
Live where you fear to live.
— Rumi

3 things I am working on changing

-
-
-

3 ways others appreciate me

-
-
-

Resist comparing your insides to other people's outsides. You are seeing only the parts they want you to see.

Assume instead that people are much more like you than different from you. We all love, hurt, dream, fear, and yearn.

What if we are all perfect in our magnificence and our fragility?

— Lara Willing

3 things that have changed my life

-
-
-

3 risks I am willing to take

-
-
-

I am only one,
but I am one.
I can not do
everything, but I
can do
something.
I must not fail
to do the
something that
I can do.

— Edward Everett Hale

3 things I treasure

-
-
-

3 ways I make the world a
better place

-
-
-

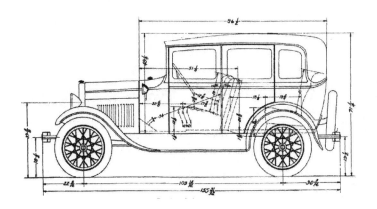

Whether you think you can or think you can't, you're right.

— Henry Ford

3 ways I take care of myself

-
-
-

3 things I can do if I'm
feeling down

-
-
-

@Lara Willing

If you are in a bad mood, go for a walk. If you are still in a bad mood, go for another walk.

— Hippocrates

3 things I am optimistic about

-
-
-

3 things I want more of

-
-
-

Three things I have learned at HAI workshops:

- People are much more like me than they are different from me.
- We all hunger for love, touch, empathy, and connection. And we can create it.
- How to listen with my heart and how good it feels to be seen and heard.

— Lara Willing

The Human Awareness Institute
www.HAI.org
since 1968

3 things I stand up against

-
-
-

3 things I forgive myself for

-
-
-

©Claudia Mariani

The wound is the place
where the light enters you.
Stay with it.
— Rumi

3 things I am passionate about

-
-
-

3 things I like just how
they are

-
-
-

Good morning, sweetheart,
I will be taking care of
everything for you today.
There is nothing you need to
worry about. I've got this!
Go out and have a good time.

Love, The Universe

3 things I say no to

-
-
-

Suffering = wanting things to be different than they are

3 ways I am moving forward

-
-
-

3 things I like about my body

-
-
-

3 things I have integrity about

-
-
-

now!

This is the perfect place at the
perfect time.
You are right where you need
to be.

3 ways I treat others well

-
-
-

3 things that bring me
pleasure

-
-
-

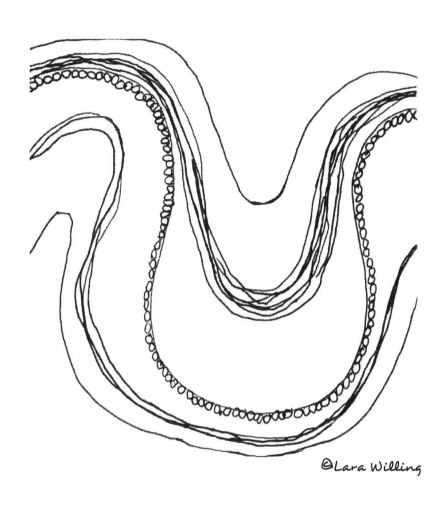

@Lara Willing

You can't stop the waves, but
you can learn to surf.
— Jon Kabat-Zinn

3 ways I could treat
myself better

-
-
-

3 things I want to get better at

-
-
-

Live as if you were to
die tomorrow.

Learn as if you were to
live forever.

Love as if you had
nothing to lose.

— adapted from
Mahatma Gandhi

3 ways I have been brave

-
-
-

3 ways I am a good friend

-
-
-

3 things that make me
come alive

-
-
-

If you want to have something different than you've ever had, you have to do something different than you've ever done.

— Thomas Jefferson

3 ways I am healing

-
-
-

3 things I wish were different

-
-
-

3 ways I am playful

-
-
-

When you are in the light,
soak it all up so you can
take it into the dark
with you.

3 things I have accomplished

-
-
-

3 things that come easily
to me

-
-
-

If you think you are too
small to make a difference,
try sleeping with a mosquito.
— Dalai Lama XIV

3 wonderful things I
absolutely deserve

-
-
-

3 ways I want to grow

-
-
-

3 things I can relax about

-
-
-

Draw what you feel right now

3 of my rules for living

-
-
-

3 things that show I have a
good life

-
-
-

3 ways I have limited myself

-
-
-

Although the world is full of suffering, it is full also of the overcoming of it.
— Helen Keller

3 things I am getting better at

-
-
-

3 ways I honor myself

-
-
-

3 things I have overcome

-
-
-

Try this practice:
Take a conscious breath and roll your shoulders.

Congratulations! You just meditated.

Repeat as needed.

3 things that make me smile

-
-
-

3 things that energize me

-
-
-

3 ways I used my body today

-
-
-

We can complain
that rose bushes
have thorns,
or rejoice that
thorn bushes have roses.
— Abraham Lincoln
(unverified author)

3 things others appreciate
about me

-
-
-

3 things I wish I could do again

-
-
-

3 ways I am creative

-
-
-

A bird
sitting in a tree is
not afraid of the
branch breaking.
Her trust is
not on the branch but
on her own wings.

— Unknown

3 things that are good for me

-
-
-

3 ways I make a difference

-
-
-

3 ways I have grown

-
-
-

©Michael Henley

"Pain is inevitable.
Suffering is optional."

3 ways I show I care

-
-
-

3 ways I stretch myself

-
-
-

Your task is not to seek for love, but merely to seek and find all the barriers within yourself that you have built against it.
— Rumi

3 things I want for others

-
-
-

3 simple things that matter

-
-
-

The sturdiest tree is not found
in the shelter of the forest
but high upon some rocky crag,
where its daily battle with the
elements shapes it into
a thing of beauty.
— Unknown

©Anne E.G. Nydam nydamprints.com

3 ways I treat myself well

-
-
-

3 ways I have fun

-
-
-

3 ways I give back

-
-
-

your love is enough

3 ways my life has improved

-
-
-

3 things I know a lot about

-
-
-

3 risks I am willing to take

-
-
-

Change will not come if we
wait for some other person or
some other time. We are the
ones we've been waiting for.
We are the change that we
seek.
— Barack Obama

3 things that feel incomplete

-
-
-

3 things I am grateful for

-
-
-

3 things that make me come
alive

-
-
-

©Lara Willing

I do not understand the mystery of grace — only that it meets us where we are and does not leave us where it found us.

— Anne Lamott

3 things I want to change
about my life

-
-
-

3 things I got done today

-
-
-

3 ways I connect
authentically

-
-
-

Remember always that you
not only have the right to be
an individual, you have an
obligation to be one.
— Eleanor Roosevelt

3 things I am working on

-
-
-

3 ways I am healing

-
-
-

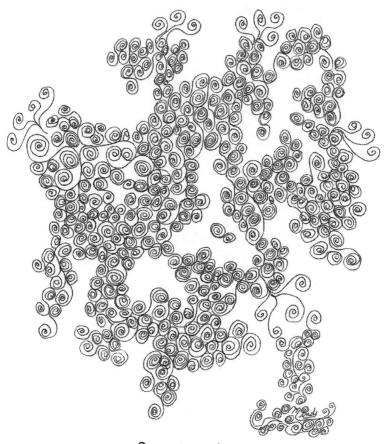

@Mindy Cutcher

You are not
a drop in the ocean.
You are
the entire ocean in a drop.
— Rumi

3 healthy habits I am building

-
-
-

3 dreams I have

-
-
-

3 things I say no to

-
-
-

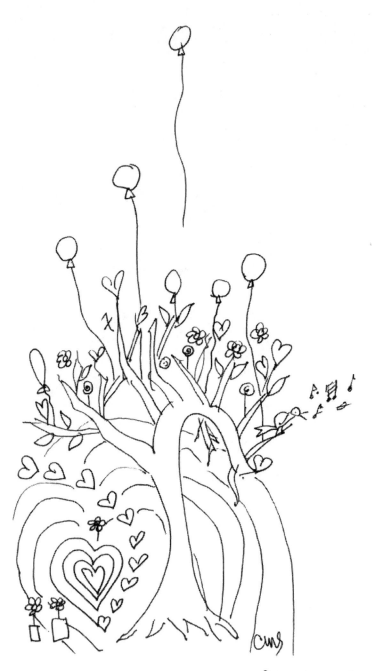

©Christine M Simpson

3 things I am ready to
leave behind

-
-
-

3 ways I have room to grow

-
-
-

Open your hands
if you want to be held.
— Rumi

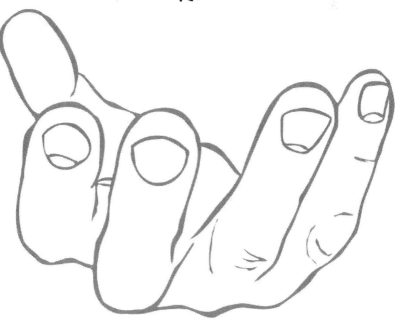

3 things I like about myself

-
-
-

3 ways I am blessed

-
-
-

You have everything you need
to take this next step.

3 ways I stretch myself

-
-
-

3 ways I am a good partner/
friend/parent

-
-
-

Don't believe everything
you think.

Make it a practice to assume
there are other explanations.

3 things I want for others

-
-
-

3 ways I am nice to my future self

-
-
-

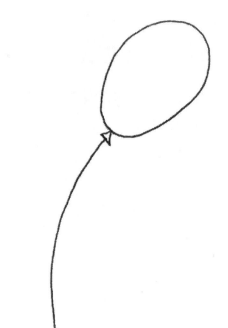

Forgiveness is letting go of
hope for a different past.

3 things I am planning for

-
-
-

3 things I wish I'd started sooner

-
-
-

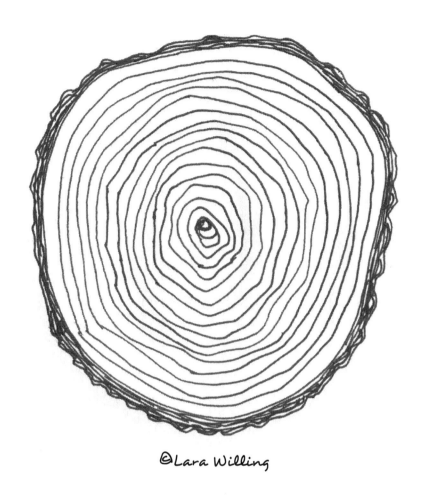

©Lara Willing

Forever is composed of nows.
— Emily Dickinson

3 things I celebrate

-
-
-

3 things I can do today to make tomorrow better

-
-
-

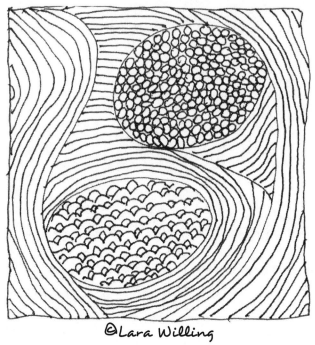

©Lara Willing

The past is gone.
Do not worship it.

The future hasn't happened yet.
Do not dwell there.

The present is a gift.
Open it, throw away the box,
and enjoy!

— Lara Willing

3 things for which I am grateful

-
-
-

3 things that have changed
my life

-
-
-

your lifelong
companion

This, above all else:
to thine own self be true.
— William Shakespeare

Thank you for including me and the **3 Things Journal** on your self-care journey. My sincere hope is that this journal has led to introspection that has enhanced your self-awareness and increased your compassion for yourself.

I encourage you to make yourself and your self-care a priority despite the pull of work, family, health or logistics. Put on your own oxygen mask first.

I wish for you a glorious balance of connection, joy, adventure, tenderness, and growth. And I believe you can have it _all_!

With care,

Cara

Credits

Art by:

Anne E.G. Nydam

Christine Simpson

Claudia Mariani

Michael Henley

Mindy Cutcher

Lara Willing

Cover design by Tera Antaree
Huge thanks to Tera for her patience
and precision with the cover and
proofreading!

Many of the art pieces were inspired by
the Zentangle Method.®

Credits

Writing by :

Quotes and poems are attributed to their author when known and are used with permission when appropriate.

All bullet point prompts, as well as unattributed quotes and tidbits are written by Lara Willing.

The interior font is Desyrel, created by Dana Rice